Fact Finders®

~ DISGUSTING HISTORY ~

The DREADFUL, SMELLY COLONIES

THE DISGUSTING DETAILS ABOUT LIFE IN COLONIAL AMERICA

by Elizabeth Raum

Consultant:
Patrick Spero
Department of History
University of Pennsylvania, Philadelphia

CAPSTONE PRESS
a capstone imprint

Fact Finders is published by Capstone Press,
151 Good Counsel Drive, P.O. Box 669, Mankato, Minnesota 56002.
www.capstonepress.com

 Books published by Capstone Press are manufactured with paper
containing at least 10 percent post-consumer waste.

Library of Congress Cataloging-in-Publication Data
Raum, Elizabeth.
    The dreadful, smelly colonies : the disgusting details about life during colonial America / by
Elizabeth Raum.
    p. cm. — (Fact finders. Disgusting history)
    Summary: "Describes disgusting details about daily life in the American Colonies, including housing,
food, and sanitation" — Provided by publisher.
    Includes bibliographical references and index.
    ISBN 978-1-4296-3959-0 (library binding)
    ISBN 978-1-4296-6351-9 (paperback)
    1. United States — Social life and customs — To 1775 — Juvenile literature. I. Title. II. Series.
E162.R39 2010
973.3 — dc22   2009029640

Editorial Credits
Christine Peterson, editor; Alison Thiele, designer; Wanda Winch, media researcher;
    Eric Manske, production specialist

Photo Credits
The Art Archive/Culver Pictures, 17; The Granger Collection, New York, cover, 14; Kathy Prenger, 13; Library
of Congress, 4 (bottom); National Parks Service/Colonial National Historical Park/Keith Rocco, artist, 19;
National Parks Service/Colonial National Historical Park/Sidney E. King, artist, 4 (top), 6, 11, 23; North Wind
Picture Archives, 9, 20, 24, 27, 29; Nova Development Corporation, 5 (all); Shutterstock/akva, (message book)
9, 17, 23; Shutterstock/freelanceartist, (design element throughout); Shutterstock/Kelpfish, 21; Shutterstock/
topal, 25; Shutterstock/Turi Tamas, (design element throughout); www.thefruitofherhands.com/Jill Howard,
10

Primary source bibliography
Page 9 — based on the writing of Thomas Prince, as published in *The Annals of New England,
    1726*, and quoted in *Woman's Life in Colonial Days* by Carl Holliday (Mineola, N.Y.:
    Dover, 1999).
Page 17 — as published in *Children in Colonial America* edited by James Marten (New York: New
    York University Press, 2007).
Page 23 — from *The American Heritage History of the Thirteen Colonies* by Louis B. Wright (New York:
    American Heritage, 1967).

Printed in the United States of America in North Mankato, Minnesota.
122010   006036R

TABLE OF CONTENTS

THE 13 AMERICAN COLONIES
1607–1776

1585
First English colony formed at Roanoke Island; it is deserted sometime before 1600.

1607 PAGE 6
Jamestown and Sagadahoc established; Sagadahoc settlement fails.

PAGE 16 **1619**
Twenty Africans arrive at Jamestown on a Dutch ship to be sold as servants.

ESTIMATED POPULATION OF COLONISTS IN AMERICA

	NUMBER OF COLONISTS	LARGEST CITY
1587	120	None
1617	4,000	None
1650	50,400	Boston – 2,000
1700s	275,000	Boston – 7,000
1720s	475,000	Boston – 12,000
1760s	1,500,000	Philadelphia – 19,000
1770s	2,210,000	Philadelphia – 28,000

PAGE 9 **1620**
About 100 colonists arrive on the *Mayflower* to form Plymouth Colony in Massachusetts.

1664
Maryland passes a law requiring lifelong slavery for Africans brought to the colonies as servants.

WILLIAM BRADFORD ON THE MAYFLOWER'S ARRIVAL IN 1620

"The whole country, full of woods and thickets, represented a wild and savage hue."

From *Of Plymouth Plantation, 1620-1647*

1630
John Winthrop arrives in Massachusetts with 900 Puritans to form Massachusetts Bay Colony with Boston as its headquarters.

PAGE 26 **1675-1676**
King Phillip's War between colonists and American Indians in New England results in the deaths of 600 English colonists and 3,000 American Indians.

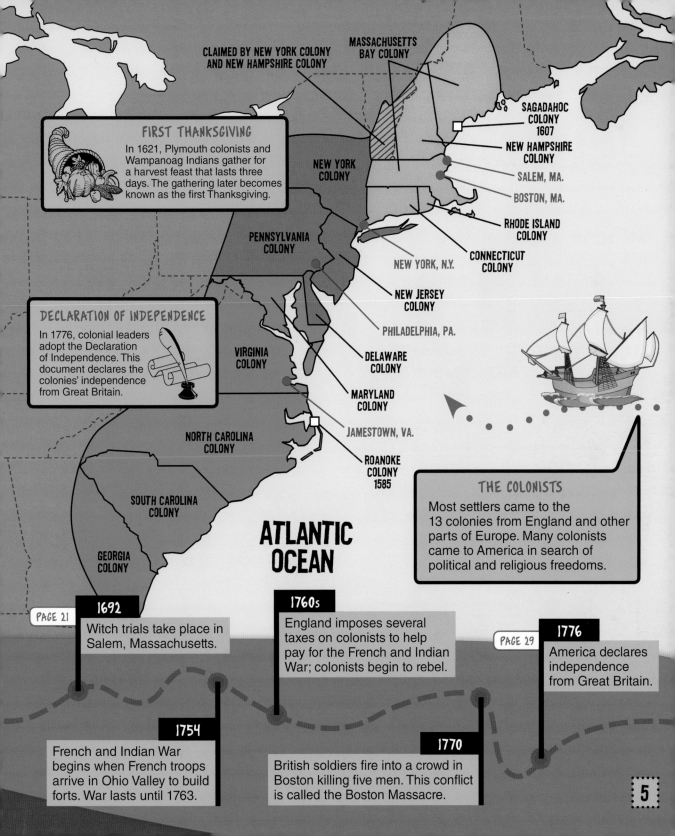

CLAIMED BY NEW YORK COLONY
AND NEW HAMPSHIRE COLONY

MASSACHUSETTS
BAY COLONY

SAGADAHOC
COLONY
1607

NEW HAMPSHIRE
COLONY

SALEM, MA.

BOSTON, MA.

NEW YORK
COLONY

RHODE ISLAND
COLONY

CONNECTICUT
COLONY

FIRST THANKSGIVING

In 1621, Plymouth colonists and Wampanoag Indians gather for a harvest feast that lasts three days. The gathering later becomes known as the first Thanksgiving.

PENNSYLVANIA
COLONY

NEW YORK, N.Y.

NEW JERSEY
COLONY

PHILADELPHIA, PA.

DECLARATION OF INDEPENDENCE

In 1776, colonial leaders adopt the Declaration of Independence. This document declares the colonies' independence from Great Britain.

VIRGINIA
COLONY

DELAWARE
COLONY

MARYLAND
COLONY

JAMESTOWN, VA.

NORTH CAROLINA
COLONY

ROANOKE
COLONY
1585

THE COLONISTS

Most settlers came to the 13 colonies from England and other parts of Europe. Many colonists came to America in search of political and religious freedoms.

SOUTH CAROLINA
COLONY

ATLANTIC OCEAN

GEORGIA
COLONY

PAGE 21

1692
Witch trials take place in Salem, Massachusetts.

1760s
England imposes several taxes on colonists to help pay for the French and Indian War; colonists begin to rebel.

PAGE 29

1776
America declares independence from Great Britain.

1754
French and Indian War begins when French troops arrive in Ohio Valley to build forts. War lasts until 1763.

1770
British soldiers fire into a crowd in Boston killing five men. This conflict is called the Boston Massacre.

FOUL FACT

In 1610, 175 new settlers arrived at Jamestown, Virginia. They found only 60 of the first 500 colonists alive. Disease and starvation had killed the rest.

When colonists arrived in America, they had to clear land and build shelters.

NEW LAND, NEW HOME

In the 1600s, colonists came to America from Europe with the hopes of freedom and a new beginning. What they found instead was rough land, harsh weather, and dreadful living conditions. When colonists arrived in America, no warm, cozy homes were waiting for them. So they needed to find shelter — fast.

In the southern colonies, the first colonists lived in tents made of sailcloth. They complained bitterly of the bugs. Mosquitoes feasted on the new arrivals.

Other colonists built small **wigwams**. They tied poles together and covered them with bark and tree branches to keep out the winter's cold. A fire added light, heat, and blinding smoke. In winter, families huddled on the straw floor beneath furs and blankets.

wigwam: a round house covered with tree bark

Some settlers in Massachusetts, New York, and Pennsylvania dug cavelike homes. They lined dirt walls with sticks to prevent the home from collapsing. One wall contained a small door. Bugs skittered in through the tree-branch roof and dropped onto sleepers. Mice, rats, and snakes slithered through the sod.

The first wooden houses were only about 20 feet (6 meters) wide by 20 feet (6 meters) long. Shutters over the windows kept out the wind, but they also kept out the light. A fire burned constantly to provide light and heat. Everyone ate, worked, and slept in just one room. A lucky family might have a table and one or two chairs. Children stood while they ate their meals. They slept on the floor on mattresses stuffed with rags, cornhusks, or bits of leftover wool. Houses smelled of smoke, stew, and sweaty bodies.

Disease and Death

March 24, 1621 – Plymouth Colony

This month thirteen of our number died. During the last three months, half of those in our colony have perished. Most died from lack of housing. Some suffered from diseases like scurvy, brought on by the long ocean voyage. Of 100 persons, scarcely 50 remain. The living are barely able to bury the dead. There is no one to care for the ill. But spring is coming, and we hope that the deaths will cease and that the sick and lame will recover. All have shown great patience during this time of suffering.

Above quotation is based on the writing of Thomas Prince, as published in The Annals of New England, 1726.

HARDTACK, ANYONE?

Picky eaters didn't last long in the colonies. At first, colonists ate what they brought with them on the ship. They ate dried peas that had to be soaked in water for hours and then boiled. For meat, they had salted pork or beef. When meat became moldy and rotten, colonists scraped away the mold and ate what was left. Their only bread was hardtack, a rock-hard cracker made of flour and water. Beetles called weevils burrowed into the hardtack, which made it easier to eat.

After these supplies ran out, most colonies suffered through a starving time. Some settlers survived on corn that they bought from American Indians. Others tried fishing. The forests were full of wildlife, but most colonists didn't own guns. So they ate whatever they could gather or kill. One Jamestown colonist reported eating "dogs, cats, rats, snakes, toadstools, horsehides, and what not." He was lucky. Many others starved.

HARDTACK

When crops were good, colonists had plenty of food to eat.

In time, colonists learned to grow corn. But corn made for a boring diet. In many homes, colonists ate cornmeal mush or porridge for both breakfast and supper. The biggest meal was often a stew of beans, corn, and other vegetables. On a good day, the stew might include raccoon or deer meat. Yum!

NO PRIVACY IN THE PRIVY

Imagine the nice, comfy bathroom you use every day. Now picture a rough tree, dirty pit, or smelly outhouse. Pretty gross, right? But that's what colonists used for bathrooms.

At first, colonists stepped behind a tree or a bush when they needed to go. But as towns grew and people lived closer together, they needed another solution.

Colonists dug pits downhill from their homes and built outhouses or privies over the pit. A board with a hole in the middle formed the seat. Waste fell into the pit. When the pit was full, colonists dug a new pit and moved the outhouse.

People who were very old or sick used a chamber pot. This pottery bowl was dumped outside each morning. Children often did this job. In cities, chamber pots were emptied into the streets, sometimes landing on people passing by.

Animals added to the problem too. Pigs, cows, and horses wandered freely through towns leaving their droppings behind. If colonists didn't watch their steps, they'd carry the stinky mess inside on their shoes.

FOUL FACT

There was no toilet paper in colonial America. Colonists used corncobs to clean themselves. They tossed them in the pit after use.

Most colonial outhouses were small wooden shacks with no windows.

DIRTY JOBS

How would you like to bend over 6,000 times a day planting tiny seeds? Sound like fun? Maybe not to you, but that's how colonists planted their crops.

But before colonists could plant seeds, they had to clear dense forest to make farm fields. Men swung heavy axes to cut down massive trees. Once the huge trees fell, they had to be cut apart and moved. There were no sawmills, so men chopped logs and firewood by hand.

Once the trees were gone, the dirty fieldwork continued. Men, women, and children used hoes and shovels to break up the hard soil. The dirty job got a little easier when plows were invented in the 1670s.

After the fields were plowed, it was time to plant. But that just meant more long hours digging in the dirt. American Indians taught colonists how to plant corn in small hills. Men and women planted corn crops by hand. They used a small stick or their finger to make holes in the dirt for corn seed.

Colonial children worked alongside their parents harvesting crops.

HARD LABOR

Colonial farms needed workers, as did businesses such as lumber and shipbuilding. **Indentured servants** and slaves did much of the work. Indentured servants signed contracts promising to work for four to seven years in exchange for a free trip to America.

In 1619 the first African slaves arrived at Jamestown. At first, a few were able to buy their freedom. Later, the laws changed making them slaves permanently. Slaves were considered the owner's property. Trying to escape meant death. Many slaves were beaten, whipped, and worked to death on the farms of colonial America.

Indentured servants and slaves got up at dawn and worked until bedtime. Female servants hauled water, cooked meals, cared for children, and helped in the fields. Male servants cleared land, tended crops, and whatever else their masters required.

indentured servant: someone who agrees to work for another person for a certain length of time in exchange for travel

COLONIAL SLAVE AUCTION

Young Slave

When I was nine, I was forced to work even harder. In summer I pounded four bushels of ears of corn every night in a barrel for the chickens. In winter I had to card wool until a very late hour. If I failed at these tasks, I would be harshly punished.

Slave boy in Massachusetts, 1740s

ROUGH ROADS

Getting around the colonies was a chore. The best way to travel was by boat, provided your craft didn't topple over in the churning waters.

Most colonists traveled by foot following old Indian trails through the woods. Trees and bushes barred the way. Travelers jumped or waded across narrow streams. They crossed deep rivers and streams in boats or canoes. Most people couldn't swim.

Carriages and carts were rare. In 1697, Philadelphia had only 30 wheeled vehicles in the entire city. Small, cramped carriages bounced along rough dirt roads. Wheels fell off. Horses got tired. A carriage trip was slow, dusty, and uncomfortable.

Long trips took several days. In remote areas, travelers slept outdoors or stayed with farm families. In towns, they stopped at taverns. The tavern owner provided food, drink, and a shared bed for a price.

In the colonies, people traveled along rough roads to buy or trade goods.

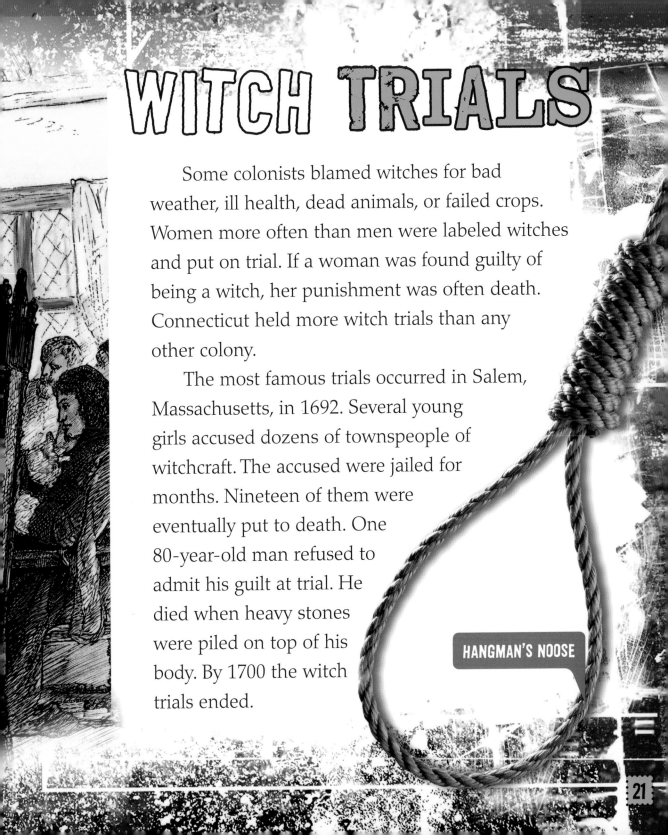

WITCH TRIALS

Some colonists blamed witches for bad weather, ill health, dead animals, or failed crops. Women more often than men were labeled witches and put on trial. If a woman was found guilty of being a witch, her punishment was often death. Connecticut held more witch trials than any other colony.

The most famous trials occurred in Salem, Massachusetts, in 1692. Several young girls accused dozens of townspeople of witchcraft. The accused were jailed for months. Nineteen of them were eventually put to death. One 80-year-old man refused to admit his guilt at trial. He died when heavy stones were piled on top of his body. By 1700 the witch trials ended.

HANGMAN'S NOOSE

BAD MEDICINE

Almost from the time they landed in America, colonists battled new and deadly diseases. **Smallpox**, diphtheria, and yellow fever killed thousands. Smallpox attacked American Indians and colonists alike. After three or four days of fever, blisters broke out all over the body. Skin fell away, and the victims died in terrible pain. Diphtheria was a deadly lung disease. Yellow fever, spread by mosquitoes, caused high fever and death.

Doctors tried bleeding patients to cure these and other illnesses. A doctor made tiny cuts in the patient's arm until blood ran freely.

Doctors also gave foul-tasting medicines that caused vomiting or diarrhea. Doctors believed that blood, vomit, and diarrhea carried illnesses away.

For fever, colonial doctors cut fish called herrings down the back and tied them to their patients' feet. Other doctors gave patients a broth made of boiled toads. People believed that the stronger the smell, the better the medicine.

smallpox: a disease that spreads easily, causing chills, fever, and pimples that scar

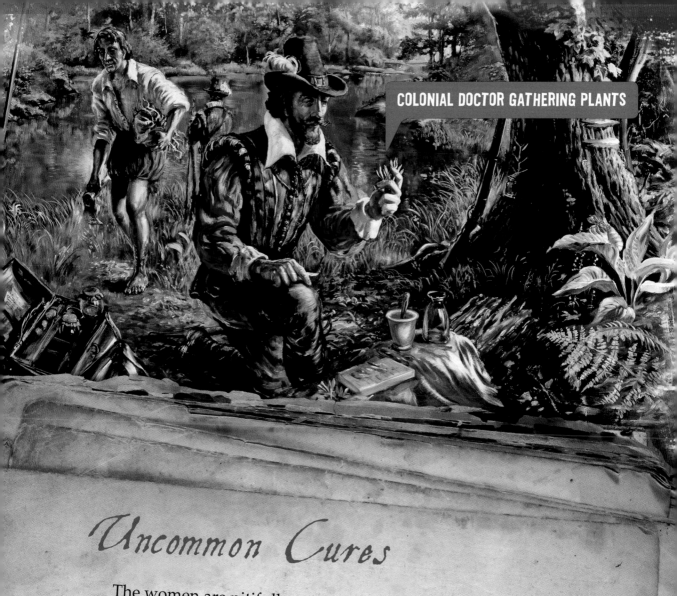

COLONIAL DOCTOR GATHERING PLANTS

Uncommon Cures

The women are pitifully tooth-shaken; whether through the coldness of the climate, or by sweetmeats [sugar], I am not sure. For toothache, I have found the following medicine very available – add butter to gunpowder and rub the jaw with it. For frozen limbs, make a lotion of soap, salt, and molasses or use cow dung boiled in milk.

John Josselyn, 1674

Colonists used hard soap and a washboard to do laundry.

WHAT'S THAT SMELL?

It wasn't just the medicines that smelled bad. Colonial people did too. They seldom bathed. Most people believed water was unhealthy. They thought the dirt and sweat caked into their skin protected them from illness. After finally taking a bath, one colonial woman said, "I bore it rather well, not having been wet all over for 28 years."

Most colonists had dirty hands, muddy feet, and greasy hair. Lice and nits crawled through colonists' hair and jumped from one person to another. Some colonists used fine combs to remove the nits. Others dusted their hair with powder. Most colonists just scratched.

Even so, people took great care to clean their clothes. Most only had two or three outfits, so keeping them clean wasn't easy. Women hauled water, heated it, and then scrubbed clothes by hand. During the winter, laundry piled up for weeks because the water froze. Most people were forced to wear dirty clothes covered with food splatters, animal droppings, and grime.

COLONIAL WATER BUCKET

DIFFICULT TIMES

Thanks to help from American Indian tribes, hearty colonists survived their first years in America. Indians taught colonists such useful skills as turning animal furs into clothing and carving dugout canoes. Even so, disputes arose over land and hunting grounds. When several Virginia tribes killed 347 colonists in 1622, colonists built forts and gathered weapons to protect themselves.

American Indians attacked small groups of settlers, using surprise as a weapon. Colonial leaders sought revenge without bothering to find out which tribe had attacked them or why. They struck out at the nearest village. Colonists used guns to kill the people and then destroyed their homes and crops.

In Massachusetts, colonists wiped out entire American Indian villages during the Pequot War of 1637. A few years later, in King Philip's War (1675-1676), American Indians burned colonial villages to the ground. Women and children were taken captive. Men were killed.

Disputes over land caused conflicts between colonists and American Indians.

TIMES CHANGE, SMELL REMAINS

Colonial life changed greatly in the years following the founding of Jamestown. Houses became larger. Many were built of brick. Brick houses didn't burn as easily as wood, and they lasted longer. Gardens flourished, and food was plentiful.

People still worked hard, but it was easier to find food and shelter. By the mid-1700s, there were stores, libraries, and mail service throughout the 13 colonies. Children attended schools. Stagecoaches carried people from place to place on well-worn roads. Newspapers provided current information.

But the colonies still smelled bad. People dumped their garbage in pits outside or burned it. Cows grazed on Boston Common. Pigs ran through the streets of New York City. Horses, cows, sheep, and chickens shared the streets with pigs and people.

Farm animals often roamed the streets of colonial towns.

Houses smelled of smoke and cooking odors. Even the fanciest homes did not have running water or indoor plumbing. Everyone used privies or outhouses, and most people still did not bathe.

Despite some smelly problems, the colonies were developing into a new country. In 1776 the 13 colonies declared their independence from Great Britain. They would soon become the United States of America.

GLOSSARY

colonist (KAH-luh-nist) — a person who comes from another country and settles in a new area

diphtheria (dif-THEER-ee-uh) — a disease that causes a high fever, weakness, and difficulties in breathing

indentured servant (in-DEN-churd SUR-vuhnt) — someone who agrees to work for another person for a certain length of time in exchange for travel expenses, food, or housing

scurvy (SKUR-vee) — a deadly disease caused by lack of vitamin C; scurvy produces swollen limbs, bleeding gums, and weakness.

smallpox (SMAWL-poks) — a disease that spreads easily from person to person, causing chills, fever, and pimples that scar

starve (STARV) — to suffer or die from lack of food

tribe (TRIBE) — a group of people who live in the same area, speak the same language, and obey the same chief

wigwam (WIG-wahm) — a round house covered with tree bark

witchcraft (WICH-kraft) — the art or practices of a person believed to be a witch

READ MORE

Fradin, Dennis B. *Jamestown, Virginia*. Turning Points in U.S. History. New York: Benchmark, 2007.

Herr, Melody. *Exploring the New World: An Interactive History Adventure*. You Choose Books. Mankato, Minn.: Capstone Press, 2008.

McNeese, Tim. *Colonial America, 1543-1763*. Discovering U.S. History. New York: Chelsea House, 2009.

Sherman, Patrice. *How'd They Do That in Colonial America?* How'd They Do That? Hockessin, Del.: Mitchell Lane, 2010.

INTERNET SITES

FactHound offers a safe, fun way to find Internet sites related to this book. All of the sites on FactHound have been researched by our staff.

Here's all you do:

Visit *www.facthound.com*

FactHound will fetch the best sites for you!

INDEX